AF350720

FOR HER

MADISON PERKINS

For Her copyright 2026 by Madison Perkins
All rights reserved. Printed in the United States of America. No part of this book may be used or reproduced in any matter whatsoever without written permission except in the case of reprints in the context of reviews.

ISBN: 979-8-234-00883-1

Gratitude—

Luna, for being my light.

Leanna, for guiding me back.

I realized staying meant silencing my story, so here it is...

In the beginning—
rain falling
falling more and more for you
cozy weather
cozied up with you
sky blanketed in clouds
bundled, blanketed with you
safe space, safe place
safe with you

When I lay wrapped in his
arms I look up and think
there's no way he'd hurt me
then I'm proved wrong
over and over again

I wanted to share a life but how
could I when I feared sharing a
feeling, a thought
weaponized vulnerabilities
left me constantly distraught

He thought I was pretty
but knew I could fly
so he locked me in a cage
and told me pretty lies

Brick by brick
he builds me up
only to break me down
pick pick pick
I feel so small
then questioned why
I put up my walls

Lost in you
longing for me
lost myself in
loving you

Give all of me for you to take
so I can't feel as my heart breaks
shattered heart, I am numb
your lie-filled words I succumbed
all they were, merely a distraction
I never noticed the lack of action

Words sweet as honey
but oh how they're sticky
stuck in my head
buzz buzz buzz
lies lies lies
they masked the stings
which complicated things
a worker harming their queen
leaving her not knowing
how to be

Words that struck
and have always stayed stuck—
'you're easier to fuck with
than to fuck'

He lights me up
then burns me down
my thoughts gasoline
and I have drowned
up in flames
an internal explosion
leading to persistent
corrosion

The coldness of lying next
to the one you love
who doesn't see your pain
doesn't hear your cries
doesn't feel you shake
instead they're peacefully
sound asleep,
that pain runs deep

Trying to escape a
confusing maze
what feels like years
has only been days

Glass half empty or half full?
mine was overflowing
pouring all my love and energy
they take, take, take
drink, drink, drink
left fully drained

We are a thousand piece
jigsaw forcing pieces where
they don't belong
impossible to complete
left feeling puzzled

Mirrored toxicity
mistaken for electric chemistry

He sets my mind on fire
it's become a liar
made to feel crazy
all memories become hazy
all the blame,
brain up in flames
he puts it out
to put me down
extinguishes then ignites

Fingers on my throat
but it was only a joke

Drowning after years
of the same cycle
— brainwash

The drinker paired
with the over-thinker
the gaslighter,
the internal fighter

The hollowness in his
eyes still haunts me

Reeling me in with bait
songs, messages, promises of
change and as soon as I'm
hooked he tosses me back to
the cold current drowning all
over again

How do I look her in the eyes
the one who gave me life
and tell her I don't want it

In the kitchen, block of knives
warm arms around her turned cold as
ice with a motion behind her back
In that moment he pierced her heart
frozen, fear all-consuming
looking into the blackness in his eyes
He would never, crazy girl.
Shouldn't she know it's only play?
The final act, the breaking point,
her reason not to stay

Constantly on edge
so close to the ledge

I want to heal and let you
heal too so we can stop
hurting and hurting each
other too
all I wanted was to love you
I just wanted you

I see it in his eyes
hear it in his tone
he's gone again
resentment sinks in
flashing back- unsettled, unsafe
oh but when he comes back,
his love for me
— intoxicating

‘I’m just trying to tame you’

I don't trust her
the emotions she feels
the thoughts she thinks
the decisions she makes
the love she gives
the hand she takes

Emotionally hostage,
internal warfare

The contradiction of
wanting to fully live and
not live at all, all at a once
but here I am
torn between going all in
or all out

Too independent,
too sensitive,
too stubborn
always too much
but somehow never enough

Doctor after doctor
none of them could find
the damages he left behind
brain scans, heart tests
none of them could read
a broken spirit,
a broken mind

Floating through the day
I don't want to stay
— dissassociation

The paradox of loving
them as a person but not
trusting them as a partner

She kept me safe
she kept me alive
she was my reason
through all the darkness
she was my light
— my Luna

I used to hope for death
because that felt easier
than leaving

Which is deceiving me,
my deep-thinking mind
or long-loving heart?
Both have steered me wrong
Torn in two,
they're fighting over what to do
one of them really wants you...

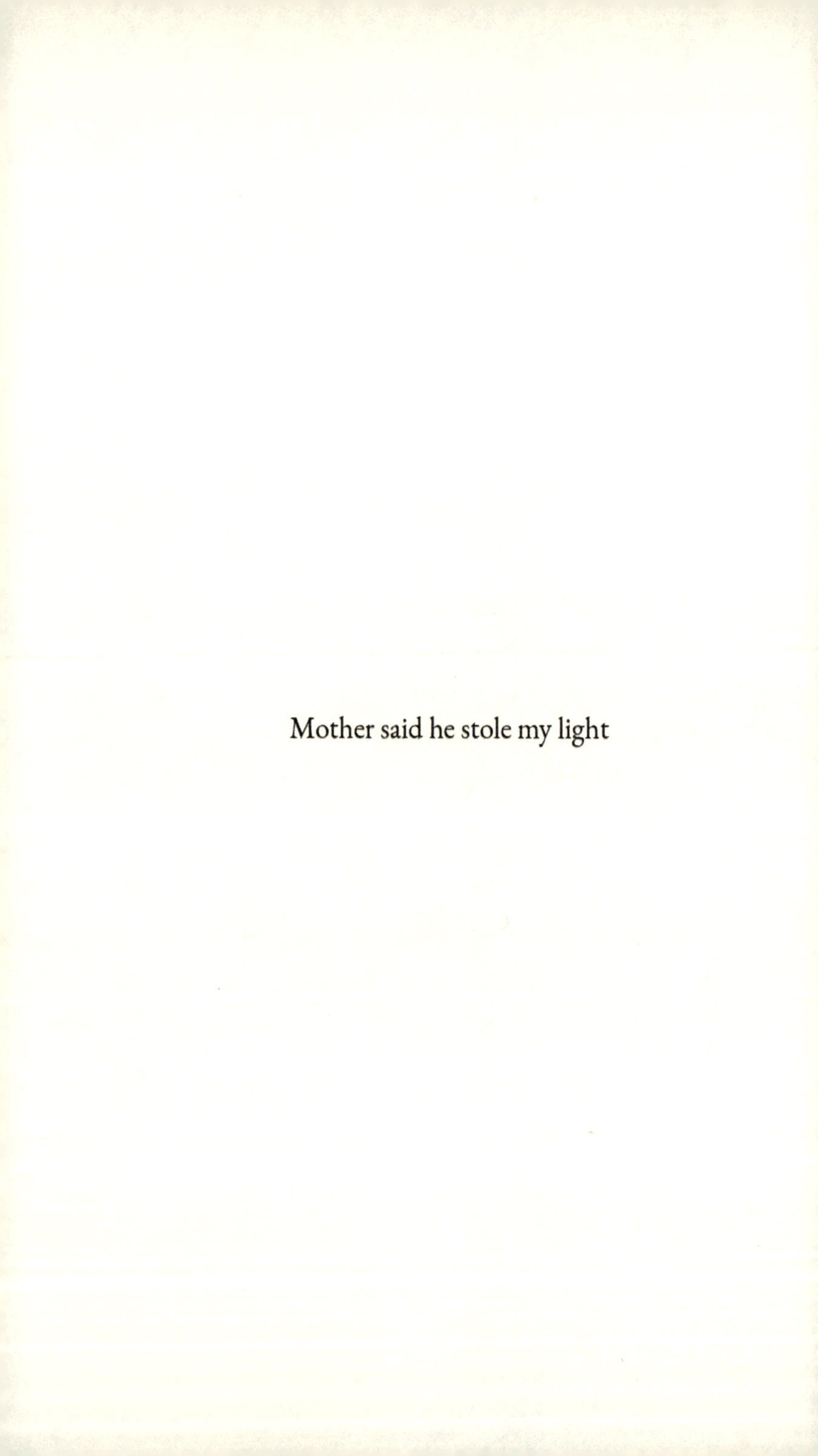
Mother said he stole my light

His last hold on me,
the triangulation
mental form
of strangulation

I was the one to walk away
but he broke my heart
time and time again until
there were no pieces left
for me to love him with

Did I stay too long
or give up too quick?
— ambivalence

His addiction makes me
want to, need to leave
but the irony is found
in my inability to quit my
addiction to him

Always told
fight for love, never give it up
but you shouldn't have to
fight so hard to be seen
to be heard, to be loved
How can one accept a love that feels
like giving up on themselves

Never beaten but no one
understands how hard his
words hit, a constant
reverberation on my mind

Twenty-something years old
two beds, same home
two kids playing house
turned into cat chasing mouse

I see all the good in him
I've seen and experienced all
the bad too
his hurt and my hurt and
how we hurt each other
looking past it
still holding love for him
but incapable of loving him
and myself at the same time

I am the secondhand product
of his father's abuse

I feared his death more
than my soul's so I stayed
and I hoped and I silently
suffered. I loved him and
lived for him and longed
for him for far too long

These broken words
within empty vow books

His well-being became
my entirety
I sacrificed my own
until I had to let go
I still hope he's held
onto his sobriety...
out of my control

He only ever saw my worth
when I walked away
so lesson learned,
I got burned
my path of self-destruction
would have been choosing to
stay

Him choosing her
broke the last pieces in me
allowing me to break free

One too many relapses
when hearing their name
feels like withdrawal

The loss of him felt so heavy
because he became such a big
part of who I was
— codependency

Reminder —
it was abuse,
his words the noose

In the quiet moments
good memories flood my mind
and as painful as it is
I sit with them before they get
left behind

The duality of
experiencing their shadow
through substance but
knowing their heart
— the most painful part

The freedom of no longer being
the target of their projected pain

A piece of me will love him
forever but we can no longer be
tethered
— cord cutting

This time ending it made me feel
like my life could finally begin

My defiance to the pain
and self pity will be found
in the alchemy of my
kindness and self-mastery

One day out of the blue
I realized I'm no longer holding
onto the hopes of me and you
with a heart less heavy,
mind less cloudy,
I carry dreams of a future not tied
to us two
No desire for revenge
just release
because I have returned to myself
and am fully at peace

All that remains is gratitude for
the reciprocity of love shared
outside the hurt caused and for
the immense growth that
ultimately led to self discovery
— my greatest catalyst

About the book —
FOR HER, a collection spanning years
navigating mental health challenges through a
tumultuous relationship. A compilation of
grief and growth, loss and reclamation of self.

About the author —
Madison is a multidimensional artist who
thrives on creating spaces where people feel
seen, valued and empowered. Through her
creative pursuits, she seeks to inspire others
and cultivate a kind community.

www.ingramcontent.com/pod-product-compliance
Lightning Source LLC
Chambersburg PA
CBHW021343160726
47994CB00007B/2837